The Wild Side of Pet
Guinea Pigs

Jo Waters

Raintree

www.raintreepublishers.co.uk
Visit our website to find out more information about **Raintree** books.

To order:
 Phone 44 (0) 1865 888112
 Send a fax to 44 (0) 1865 314091
Visit the Raintree Bookshop at **www.raintreepublishers.co.uk** to browse our catalogue and order online.

First published in Great Britain by Raintree, Halley Court, Jordan Hill, Oxford OX2 8EJ, part of Harcourt Education.
Raintree is a registered trademark of Harcourt Education Ltd.

Editorial: Melanie Copland and Saskia Besier
Design: Richard Parker and
Tinstar Design Ltd (www.tinstar.co.uk)
Picture Research: Maria Joannou and Alison Prior
Production: Duncan Gilbert

Originated by Ambassador Litho Ltd
Printed and bound in China by South China Printing Company

The paper used to print this book comes from sustainable resources.

ISBN 1 844 43483 4
08 07 06 05 04
10 9 8 7 6 5 4 3 2 1

British Library Cataloguing in Publication Data
Waters, Jo
The Wild Side of Pet Guinea Pigs
636.9'3592
A full catalogue record for this book is available from the British Library.

Acknowledgements
The publishers would like to thank the following for permission to reproduce photographs: Ardea pp. **5 top** (Ken Lucas), **14** (H beste), **16**, **27** (J Daniels); Art Directors & Trip p. **25** (B Gibbs); Bruce Coleman Collection pp. **22** (Jane Burton), **23** (J Wegner), **29** (Hans Reinhard), **26**; Dave Bradford p. **12**; FLPA p. **28** (Foto Natura Stock/W Meinderts); Nature Picture Library pp. **4** (P Johnson), **10** (P Oxford), **24** (Jim Clare); Oxford Scientific Films pp. **6** (C Catton), **19** (H Reinhard), **13**, **21** (J Kleine & M Hubert), **20** (D Bartlett); Tudor photography/Harcourt Education Ltd pp. **5 bot**, **7**, **9**, **11**, **15**, **17**.

Cover photograph of a pet guinea pig, reproduced with permission of Tudor Photography/ Harcourt Education Ltd. Inset cover photograph of a rock cavy reproduced with permission of FLPA (Minden Pictures/Claus Meyer).

The publishers would like to thank Michaela Miller for her assistance in the preparation of this book.

Every effort has been made to contact copyright holders of any material reproduced in this book. Any omissions will be rectified in subsequent printings if notice is given to the publishers.

Contents

Any words appearing in bold, **like this**, are explained in the Glossary.

Was your pet once wild?

Did you know that your pet guinea pig is actually closely related to wild animals? Finding out more about your guinea pig's wild **ancestors** will help you give it a better life.

Rodents

Guinea pigs are actually small **rodents**, like mice, rats and squirrels. Wild guinea pigs are often called cavies. Many of them are very like the guinea pigs we keep as pets.

The Patagonian cavy is the biggest wild cavy.

Pet guinea pigs are usually friendly and love company. Guinea pigs do not need walking as they can exercise in your home and garden and their cage. They do need quite a lot of looking after but this can be great fun.

Pet guinea pigs are very like some of their wild relatives.

Pets

Guinea pigs have been kept in Britain for over 400 years.
Domestic *guinea pigs were bred from wild guinea pigs. Explorers brought them to Europe from South America in the 1500s. Queen Elizabeth I owned a guinea pig.*

Types of guinea pig

Wild cavies are short, stocky animals with small, round ears. They usually have no visible tail. Most cavies look similar but they can be different sizes.

Cavy types

The common Brazilian cavy is about half the size of a pet guinea pig. Yellow-toothed cavies are small and stocky. They get their name from their yellowy-orange teeth. Rock cavies live in rocky mountains. They have blunt claws.

Capybaras live in South America.

Giant guinea pigs

Guinea pigs are related to capybaras. Capybaras can grow over a metre long and love the water.

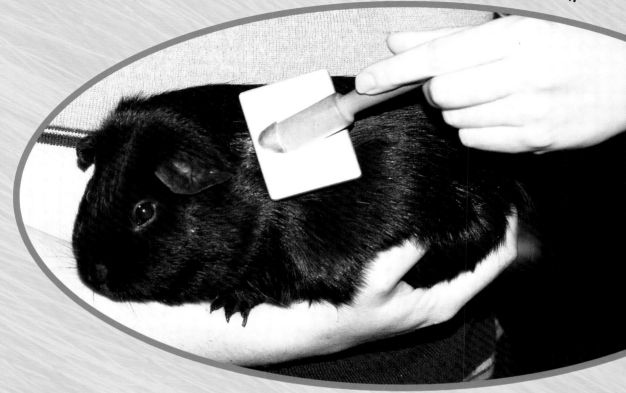

Guinea pigs like to be brushed often.

There are three main types of pet guinea pig.
There are shorthaired guinea pigs such as English,
American or Bolivian, longhairs like Peruvians and
rough-hairs like Abyssinians.

Allergies

Some people cannot keep guinea pigs because they
are **allergic** to their hairs. You should make sure
that nobody in your family has an allergy before
you decide to get a guinea pig.

Where are guinea pigs from?

Wild cavies are found all over South America. Brazilian cavies live wild across much of Brazil. Bolivian cavies live high up in the Andes Mountains. Cavies also live wild in Columbia, Venezuela and northern Argentina.

There are old statues showing guinea pigs or cavies on the north coast of Peru.

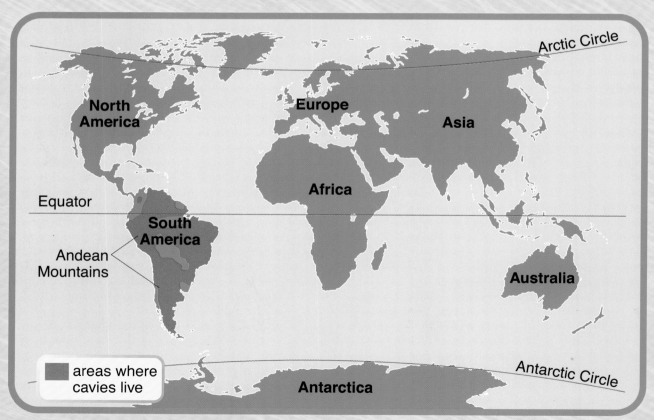

This map shows where wild cavies can be found.

Guinea pigs should be alert and full of energy.

Always buy your guinea pig from a good home. You can ask a local vet to recommend a place.

When you choose a guinea pig, make sure it has not been near any ill guinea pigs. When you try to pick it up, it should either try to run away or investigate you. It should have clean eyes, nose and bottom.

Rescue pigs

Sometimes guinea pigs lose their home through no fault of their own. Think about adopting a guinea pig from an animal centre like the RSPCA instead of buying one.

Guinea pig habitats

Wild cavies live in different sorts of **habitats**. Some live high up in the mountains. They can also live in grasslands, rocky places, swamps and forest edges.

Cavies live in **burrows**. They do not often dig, but can if they need to. They may take over an abandoned burrow.

Agouti

Cavies' coat colour is called 'agouti'. The colour changes from one end of the hair to the other.

Cavies have a grey or spotted brown coat. They use it to blend into their background of grassland.

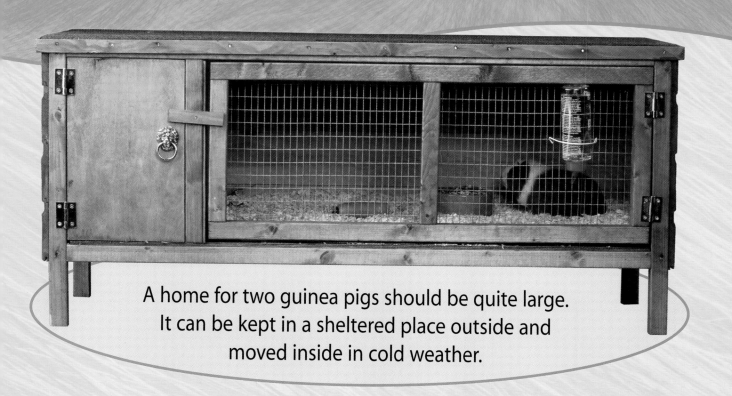

A home for two guinea pigs should be quite large. It can be kept in a sheltered place outside and moved inside in cold weather.

Your home will become your pet guinea pig's habitat. It needs a cage, which will be like the burrow it would have in the wild.

Guinea pigs need deep soft bedding, like hay, to sleep and burrow in. Underneath this there should be a 5-centimetre-deep layer of cat litter or wood chippings.

Your guinea pig's home needs to be cleaned every day and the bedding should be changed weekly.

Guinea pig anatomy

Cavies have short necks, thick bodies and large heads. Their tails are so short that they do not come outside their bodies. They have sturdy feet with four 'fingers'.

Sharp teeth

Cavies have twenty strong, sharp teeth. They use them for chewing plants. Male cavies also use their teeth in fights with other cavies. First they rattle them as a threat. Then they attack and try to bite the other cavy.

This drawing shows the skeleton of a guinea pig.

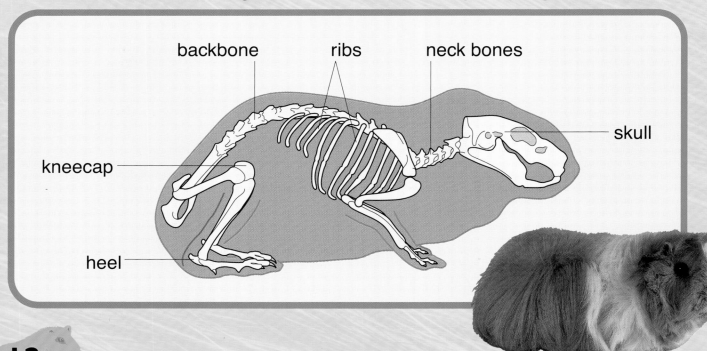

backbone   ribs   neck bones

skull

kneecap

heel

Rough-haired Abyssinians have rough swirls of hair on their backs and heads.

Pet guinea pigs have the same **anatomy**, or body parts, as their wild cousins.

Pet guinea pigs can have different length coats. Longhaired Peruvians can have coats up to 10 centimetres long. They need grooming every day. Do you have time to do this?

Pet guinea pigs cannot exercise as much as in the wild. This means that their nails need to be trimmed regularly by a vet.

Gnawing and trimming

*Guinea pigs' teeth keep growing all their lives. You should give your guinea pig a wooden block to **gnaw** on. This will stop its teeth getting too long.*

Senses

Cavies have very sensitive eyes, ears and noses. They use them to find food and avoid danger.

Cavies' eyes are set on the sides of their heads. They need all-round vision in order to watch out for **predators**.

Cavies' sense of smell is very strong. They use this sense to recognize other cavies and to find out where they are. Cavies can also hear much higher sounds than humans can.

Cavies need all their senses, because they are **prey** animals.

Pet guinea pigs also have an amazing sense of hearing. They use it to listen out for friends, including you, and dangers.

Guinea pig safety

Guinea pigs do not see in the same way as we do. Because pet guinea pigs have eyes on the sides of their heads, it is easy for them to spot dangers and predators. But it means they have difficulty judging distances. Make sure your pets cannot get on to high places, where they could fall and hurt themselves.

Movement

Cavies and guinea pigs are very quick, **agile** animals. Guinea pigs have different muscles for doing different things. They use their fast twitch muscles for speed to escape **predators**. They use slow twitch muscles for everyday eating, grooming and walking about.

Swimming

Most guinea pigs like to bathe and can swim well. Their wild relatives, such as capybaras, can spend a lot of their time in water or swampy places.

Cavies can run quickly, turn sharply and stop almost immediately, to escape predators.

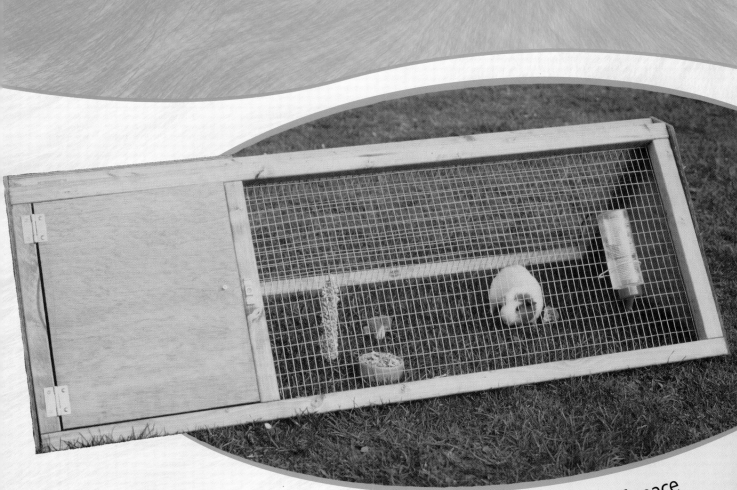

Guinea pigs like lots of space to run and a place to hide.

Cages for guinea pigs should have plenty of room for them to exercise, play and sleep.

If guinea pigs get scared, they run and hide, just as in the wild. Make sure you block any holes or spaces in your house where a guinea pig could get lost.

Handling
Pick up your guinea pig gently, with one hand under its bottom and the other around its shoulders. Guinea pigs do not like to be handled too much.

Guinea pig food

All cavies are **herbivores**. They mostly eat grasses, fruits and seeds. They can climb quite well to reach leaves from plants.

Guinea pigs have a clever way of making sure that they get all the goodness out of their food. They **digest** it twice. To do this they produce special, moist **faeces** which they then eat.

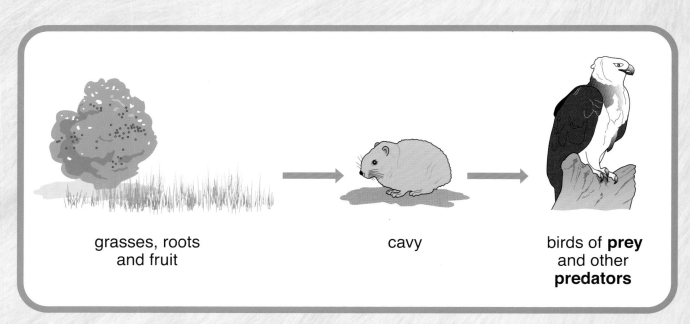

| grasses, roots and fruit | cavy | birds of **prey** and other **predators** |

Cavies fit into a **food chain** like this.

Every day guinea pigs should have 50 to 80 grams of special guinea pig food. They should also have 100 grams of a mixture of dandelion leaves, grass and raw vegetables.

Fresh foods and vitamins will help your pet stay healthy.

They should always have fresh water. A water bottle with a metal spout is best. Bowls can get tipped over or dirty.

Vitamin C

Guinea pigs need **vitamin** C every day. In the wild they get this from fresh plants. Your pet should eat fresh food, but one 250 milligram vitamin C tablet crushed and sprinkled on food or in their water will make sure they get enough.

Foraging and playing

When they are awake, wild guinea pigs are very active. They do not hunt, but run around **foraging** for fresh food. They scatter or run back to the **burrow** every so often when they sense danger. They are always alert when they are outside the burrow.

Young guinea pigs play as a way of learning. All guinea pigs are **social** and like to join in. It helps the **colony** bond together.

Cavies spend most of their time finding nice grasses and plants to eat.

Pet guinea pigs cannot get rid of their energy by foraging as they would in the wild. Playing with them every day is a good way of giving guinea pigs some exercise.

Bonding
Playing helps you bond with your guinea pigs. They will think of you as a member of their colony.

Make sure all electrical cables or valuable possessions are well out of the way. Guinea pigs will chew anything that looks interesting or tasty.

A length of tube is a good toy for guinea pigs. They also like blocks, mirrors, bells, paper sacks and old towels.

21

Living in groups

Cavies live in groups called **colonies**. There is a boss male guinea pig with a group of about ten females and babies.

Cavies are quite noisy. They use their voices to **communicate** with other members of the colony. Loud squeals warn of danger. Cooing or gentle grunts are signs that all is well.

Body language

Body language is also important. Cavies will greet each other by touching noses. If they rise up on stiff legs, it means that they are threatening another cavy. Hissing warns that they are about to attack.

Just as in the wild, pet guinea pigs need company. It is best to keep mothers and daughters, or fathers and sons together. They can fight if they live with strange guinea pigs.

Communicating

Your pet guinea pigs will communicate with you just like they would in a wild colony. They will coo or gurgle when they are petted. They will grumble if you do something they do not like, such as touching their tummy.

You should also keep males and females separate. Otherwise they will have babies.

Guinea pigs are friendly animals so it is unfair to keep one by itself.

Sleeping

*Cavies sleep during the night and some of the day. Cavies are usually most active around dawn and dusk. They use the low light to stay hidden from **predators**.*

Most cavies and guinea pigs sleep a lot. It is important for babies to get lots of sleep when they are young because it helps them grow.

Cavies sleep and rest in their **burrows**. They also have their young in their burrows.

Pet guinea pigs will be awake at
dusk and dawn, just like wild cavies.
They will want food each morning and evening.

Fitting in with daily life

Pet guinea pigs usually fit in very well with normal
daily life. They are awake in the morning just as
you get ready for school. Then they will rest
during the day and be awake again when you
come home in the evening.

Guinea pig life cycle

Cavies will live for about 4 years in the wild.

Female cavies are usually **pregnant** for about 2 months. They give birth to between one and four babies, called pups. The pups are born with fur and their eyes open.

Families

*A family of cavies will leave the **burrow** with one parent in front of the pups and the other behind so that nobody gets lost.*

This is a pregnant cavy.

Pet guinea pigs usually live from 4 to 7 years.

Guinea pig pups are cute but it can be hard to find homes for them.

Neutering

Guinea pigs can have up to five pups in a litter. It can be difficult to find new homes for guinea pigs, so it is a good idea to stop your pet from having babies. Female guinea pigs can be **neutered** to stop them getting pregnant.

Is my guinea pig pregnant?

It is difficult to tell if your guinea pig is pregnant. Your vet may be able to feel slight swellings after 3 to 4 weeks. After 5 weeks you will be able to see that she is getting fatter!

Common problems

Cavies in the wild are all hunted by other animals. Their **predators** include eagles, other birds of **prey** and wild cats. They are also killed by humans. They can be harmed by **pollution** and damage to their **habitat**.

In danger

*Cavies are not **endangered**. But if people keep destroying or polluting forests and grasslands, cavies could be harmed.*

Cavies in the wild are sometimes caught for human food!

These are some common guinea pig problems.

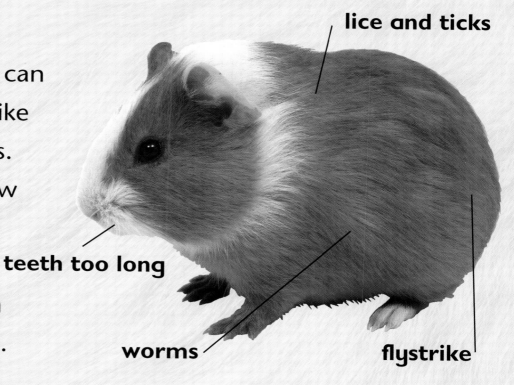

lice and ticks

Pet guinea pigs can get **parasites** like ticks and worms. Ask your vet how to treat them.

teeth too long

Guinea pigs can also get flystrike. Flies lay eggs in dirty fur. Maggots hatch out of the eggs and burrow into the guinea pig. Flystrike can kill in 24 hours, so keep your guinea pigs very clean and groom them often.

worms

flystrike

Coughs and colds

Guinea pigs can catch colds from humans. If you have a cold, you should not handle your pets.

Find out for yourself

A good owner will always want to learn more about keeping a pet guinea pig. To find out more information about guinea pigs, you can look in other books and on the Internet.

Books to read
Pets: Guinea pigs, Michaela Miller
(Heinemann Library/RSPCA, 1997)
Looking After My Pet Guinea Pig, David Alderton
(Lorenz Books, 2003)

Using the Internet
Explore the Internet to find out about guinea pigs. Websites can change, so if one of the links below no longer works, don't worry. Use a search engine, such as *www.yahooligans.com* or *www.internet4kids.com*. You could try searching with the keywords 'guinea pig', 'pet' and 'cavy'.

Websites
This pet site is full of tips, links to other sites, clubs and books: *www.petwebsite.com/guinea_pigs.asp*

The PDSA website tells you about how to care for guinea pigs: *www.pdsa.org.uk/pages/page03_4.cfm*

Glossary

agile able to move fast and easily

allergic react badly to something – you may get a rash or itch

anatomy how the body is made

ancestor animals in the past, from which today's animals come from

burrow a hole in the ground where guinea pigs sleep

colony a group of guinea pigs that live together

communicate to make yourself understood

digest break food down into pieces tiny enough to pass into blood

domestic animals that have been bred to be tame

endangered in danger of dying out or being killed

faeces the solid waste left over after food has been digested

food chain the links between different animals that feed on each other and on plants

foraging searching for food

gnaw chew, bite or nibble at something

habitat where an animal or plant lives

herbivore animal that eats only plants

mate two animals come together to make babies

neutered animal that has had an operation so it cannot have babies

parasite tiny animal that lives in or on another animal and feeds off it

pollution making places dirty with waste or poisonous chemicals

predator animal that hunts and eats other animals

pregnant to have a baby growing inside

prey animal that is hunted and eaten by other animals

rodents a group of small animals whose teeth grow all their lives

social likes company and living in groups

vitamin special chemicals that animals need to stay alive

Index

Titles in the *Wild Side of Pets* series include:

Hardback   1 844 43479 6

Hardback   1 844 43478 8

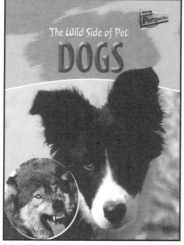

Hardback   1 844 43480 X

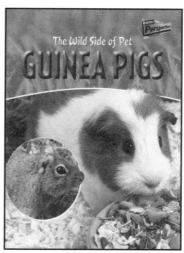

Hardback   1 844 43483 4

Hardback   1 844 43481 8

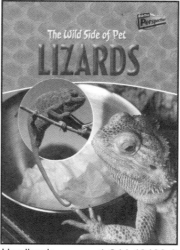

Hardback   1 844 43482 6

Find out about the other titles in this series on our website www.raintreepublishers.co.uk